The Days Are as Grass

A Collection of Eight Short Plays

Carol Hall

A Samuel French Acting Edition

SAMUELFRENCH.COM
SAMUELFRENCH-LONDON.CO.UK

Copyright © 2013 by Carol Hall. All Rights Reserved.
Cover Image © Viachaslau Kraskouski / Shutterstock

THE DAYS ARE AS GRASS is fully protected under the copyright laws of the United States of America, the British Commonwealth, including Canada, and all other countries of the Copyright Union. All rights, including professional and amateur stage productions, recitation, lecturing, public reading, motion picture, radio broadcasting, television and the rights of translation into foreign languages are strictly reserved.

ISBN 978-0-573-70114-6

Samuel French, Inc.	Samuel French Ltd.
45 West 25th Street	52 Fitzroy Street
New York, NY 10010	London W1T 5JR England
www.SamuelFrench.com	www.SamuelFrench-London.co.uk

FOR PRODUCTION INQUIRIES
Info@SamuelFrench.com
1-866-598-8449

No one shall make any changes in this play(s) for the purpose of production. No part of this book may be reproduced, stored in a retrieval system, or transmitted in any form, by any means, now known or yet to be invented, including mechanical, electronic, photocopying, recording, videotaping, or otherwise, without the prior written permission of the publisher. No one shall upload this play(s), or part of this play(s), to any social media sites.

CAUTION: Professional and amateur producers are hereby warned that *THE DAYS ARE AS GRASS* is subject to a licensing fee. The amateur and/or professional live stage performance rights to *THE DAYS ARE AS GRASS* are controlled exclusively by Samuel French, Inc. Publication of this play(s) does not imply availability for performance. Both amateurs and professionals considering a production are strongly advised to apply to Samuel French, Inc. before starting rehearsals, advertising, or booking a theatre. A Licensing fee must be paid whether the play(s) is presented for charity or gain and whether or not admission is charged. Professional/Stock and amateur licensing fees are quoted upon application to Samuel French, Inc.

Whenever the play(s) is produced the following notice must appear on all programs, printing and advertising for the play(s): "Produced by special arrangement with Samuel French, Inc."

For all motion picture, television, and other media rights: Mark Merriman, Esq., Frankfurt Kurnit Klein & Selz PC, 488 Madison Avenue, New York, NY 10022.

MUSIC USE NOTE

Licensees are solely responsible for obtaining formal written permission from copyright owners to use copyrighted music in the performance of this play and are strongly cautioned to do so. If no such permission is obtained by the licensee, then the licensee must use only original music that the licensee owns and controls. Licensees are solely responsible and liable for all music clearances and shall indemnify the copyright owners of the play(s) and their licensing agent, Samuel French, against any costs, expenses, losses and liabilities arising from the use of music by licensees.

IMPORTANT BILLING AND CREDIT REQUIREMENTS

All producers of *THE DAYS ARE AS GRASS* must give credit to the Author(s) of the Play(s) in all programs distributed in connection with performances of the Play(s), and in all instances in which the title of the Play(s) appears for the purposes of advertising, publicizing or otherwise exploiting the Play(s) and/or a production. The name of the Author(s) *must* appear on a separate line on which no other name appears, immediately following the title and *must* appear in size of type not less than fifty percent of the size of the title type.

THE DAYS ARE AS GRASS received its world premiere at the Woodstock Fringe Festival of Theatre and Song in the Byrdcliffe Theatre in Woodstock, New York in August 2004. The performance was directed by Vivian Matalon, with sets by Michael Miller, and costumes by Tracy Christiansen. All roles were performed by Brent Erdy and Nicola Sheara.

CONTENTS

Vacation 9

Last Will and Testament 15

Life Time 21

Sensations. 29

The River Jordan Lamp. 39

Jack and Jill 47

The Days Are as Grass. 53

The Last Word 67

AUTHOR'S NOTES

These eight one-act plays were written to be performed by two actors, one man and one woman. However, they can also be performed by a larger cast.

For Leonard Majzlin

VACATION

CHARACTERS

MAN - 45-50, urban, witty, tells a good story
WOMAN - 45-50, loves detail, can't get enough of it

*(A **MAN** and a **WOMAN**, in their fifties. They are at a party. We hear the ambient, muffled background sounds of conversation.)*

MAN. We had decided to fly First Class.

WOMAN. Just this once. Treat ourselves? We deserve it.

MAN. The weekend in Nassau. Leave Thursday. Come back Sunday. A quickie.

WOMAN. We deserve it.

MAN. It was while waiting to board the plane that we first noticed the couple.

WOMAN. We saw him first. How to describe? Harried executive. Slight frown between the eyebrows. Nervous. He asked the man behind the boarding desk, had a *Mrs. Pribble* arrived yet?

MAN. I was struck by the question. I don't know why. Something about the vibrating timbre of voice with which he said "Mrs. Pribble", made me feel – for some quirky reason – that this was not Mr. Pribble.

WOMAN. Then suddenly, in a flurry, Mrs. Pribble arrived. Running down the terminal passageway to meet him.

MAN. How to describe? Young.

WOMAN. Thirty-something. Running down the terminal passageway to meet him.

MAN. Up to the boarding desk. Out of breath. A little disarray. Handbag slightly unzipped, blond hair not quite in place.

WOMAN. Out of breath. But so in love!

MAN. So in love! The harried executive went to meet her, to help her with her bag. They embraced.

WOMAN. A deep kiss.

MAN. *Deep.* Then the flight was announced and everybody boarded the plane.

WOMAN. And all the way to Nassau they held hands, touched faces, kissed, fell asleep entangled. They never stopped touching.

MAN. We saw all this because they were also flying First Class. Had seats just across from us.

WOMAN. This was not Mr. Pribble. I was certain of it. I looked at her left hand. No ring. Him either.

MAN. The flight was short, and we soon arrived in Nassau, and somehow with the crowd and the baggage claim and the taxi lines and the little welcoming band playing "Yellowbird", we soon completely forgot everything except getting to our hotel.

WOMAN. As well as forgetting The Pribbles.

MAN. Or the Not-Pribbles. Mrs. Pribble and Whoever.

WOMAN. Whoever.

MAN. At any rate, it comes Sunday, and now we are back in the airline terminal waiting to go home.

WOMAN. Who should appear?

MAN. Mrs. Pribble. And the harried executive.

WOMAN. *But. Not. With. One. Another.*

MAN. No.

WOMAN. *Not. With. One. Another.*

MAN. There is someone else! There is someone else with Mrs. Pribble!

WOMAN. The someone else is Mr. Pribble.

MAN. Don't ask me how we know.

WOMAN. Well, for one thing, now she is wearing a ring.

MAN. The real Mr. Pribble is even more harried than the lover. He is getting bags, counting suitcases, buying a newspaper, checking his tickets.

WOMAN. While he does that, we watch Mrs. Pribble.

MAN. And her lover.

WOMAN. Her lover.

MAN. Yes! Because across the terminal, where at least three hundred people are waiting for several different airplanes back to the States, people who are sitting in chairs, lying on backpacks, standing in line, carrying straw bags, people whose sunburns are peeling, people who smell of Coppertone, amidst all these people, Mrs. Pribble's Harried Executive Last Thursday Lover stands alone and watches Mrs. Pribble as she sits next to her husband.

WOMAN. We see them exchange glances across the terminal. Sad glances.

MAN. And then, Mrs. Pribble's lover gets on one plane.

WOMAN. And Mrs. Pribble and her husband get on another. With us! And for one mischievous moment, I imagine myself saying to her, "Didn't we fly down together? Thursday? First Class?" But she looks so sad, I can't do it.

MAN. I'm still trying to work out the details in my mind. Was there one night of illicit love *before* the husband arrived in Nassau? On the return flight, Mrs. Pribble was tan. A beautiful bronze. The lover was golden. Mr. Pribble was pale as a sheet.

WOMAN. A sheet.

MAN. So who stayed indoors? And when? And did the real Mr. Pribble arrive Saturday morning? Saturday afternoon? *For one night only in Nassau?* He was pale as a sheet.

WOMAN. Did they all stay in the same hotel?

MAN. And here's the question: what really is the moral of this story?

WOMAN. I'll be honest. It seems to me that of everyone in this story, we are the worst.

MAN. Because we enjoyed the infidelity so much. A great deal more than they seemed to.

WOMAN. I mean, it actually added to our weekend. A real treat.

MAN. Oh, well. We deserve it.

TOGETHER. We deserve it.

LAST WILL AND TESTAMENT

CHARACTERS

WOMAN - 50, elegant, conservative, nervous perfectionist

(A well-dressed **WOMAN** *[tweeds, sensible shoes, black velvet hair band] sits at a writing desk.)*

WOMAN. Lately, I've been making out my Will. That's not as dreary as it sounds. They say you should do it when you don't actually have to. Be prepared! Just in case! You never know! Anyway. The first part seemed easy – my grandmother's brooch, a little painting given to me by my cousin, a bond or two. Simple enough.

Then I thought of something.

What I wanted to do was to recognize my friends in some way. To let them know I had…cared. That life hadn't been just school committees and yoga class and tickets to the Film Festival! I had…cared. And I wanted them all to know that. Is that too sentimental? Too morbid? I don't think so.

So. I decided that in my Will I would issue a very special invitation to a few of my closest friends, to come over right after my funeral service and pick out a little something – just a small item that would, in essence, remind them of me. I was thinking that the 18th Century green Chinese dogs on the mantelpiece might go to my friend Elisabetta, or perhaps Victor would want the Russian icon, or maybe Boomer would like the ashtray from the Marrakesh hotel. *You* know the sort of thing.

Well, instantly the whole idea went completely awry. I remembered about the Fitz-Feigans. The Fitz-Feigans (and I love them, I do, and I don't mean to be in any way judgmental, but we do have to be *realistic* here)… the Fitz-Feigans, in a nano-second, would roll up the midnight blue Art Deco carpet and carry it right out. I mean, I adore the Fitz-Feigans! However, they are like that. They do love a bargain. And after all, we're talking about a funeral, not a thrift shop.

WOMAN. *(cont.)* So. I added to the Will that my husband would need to give approval to what was being picked out by my friends.

That was when I began to worry. I didn't know how to express this delicately. Should I put into the Will that Elisabetta and Victor and Boomer can take a *tiny little item* to remember me by, but that someone in the immediate family should be sure to make certain that it isn't worth over one hundred dollars? Two hundred? And *where* is this immediate family member when he or she is making certain? At the door? With a price list?

I called my lawyer for advice. My lawyer said we're talking about a Will, not a tag sale. My lawyer said that I should simply call it a "small memento." The Fitz-Feigans and Elisabetta and Victor and Boomer could, with my husband's approval, pick out a "small memento."

That sounded rather nice. Yes. Then I began to worry again. The Fitz-Feigans have a cousin, LuEllen, whom I've always been deeply fond *of,* but not close *to,* and I began to think that LuEllen might be hurt if the Fitz-Feigans were invited to pick out a "small memento" and she *wasn't.* And then there was an additional little stickiness about the situation too because, several years before, the first husband of LuEllen had left LuEllen, to run off with a beautiful Italian girl whom the Fitz-Feigans had hired as a babysitter one summer, out at their beach house. And of course, it had not been the Fitz-Feigans' FAULT that the babysitter had been out at their beach house to be run off *with* by LuEllen's first husband, but for a while it had been quite an awkward period for us all. Eventually, we worked it out. Still. Clearly, LuEllen really should not be one of the Memento People. Am I being too harsh here?

I asked my husband what he thought. My husband said we're talking about a legal document, not a dinner party.

Also. There was the matter of Elisabetta. Elisabetta had never really recovered from the fact that her daughter is a lesbian and ours is not. I mean, really! Who cares? Nobody cares! Absolutely nobody! Nevertheless. Elisabetta had made a few remarks at my daughter's wedding. Never mind what! Just…a few remarks. I saw her over there in the corner with Boomer.

And speaking of Boomer, since he and Victor parted ways as business partners, perhaps it's asking too much of them to have them both come to pick out a small memento? They might get into some dreadful pushing and pulling thing, over the Russian icon or the ashtray from Marrakech! And the icon is so much more valuable than the ashtray. Should I add something to the ashtray? Some silver spoons?

All this made me so tired. That was when I decided to simply forego the small mementos. Kiss them goodbye. Leave everything to my immediate family.

Absolutely! Yes! Forget the Russian icon! Never mind the ashtray from Marrakesh! Screw the 18th Century green Chinese dogs!

My friends will have to *trust* that I had…cared. They will simply have to figure that out for themselves. I can't help them do it.

The details of your own mortality can be exhausting.

And I'm sure Death is no picnic either.

I finished the Will and made my husband executor. He said he hopes to God he goes before I do.

Isn't that sweet?

LIFE TIME

CHARACTERS

DADDY - 80, cheerful, easy-going
MOTHER - 80, no-nonsense

(A kitchen; messy, cluttered, too much stuff, too much dust. **DADDY**, *an old man of about 85, is seated at the rickety table. There's a sink full of dishes and above it a window, through which the sky is visible.* **MOTHER**, *also about 85, is standing in front of the sink, staring intently out the window.)*

DADDY. I woke up this mornin' feelin' just like one of them old-fashioned real long straight wooden measurin' sticks. You know the kind? Got little hinges on 'em?

*(****MOTHER*** *is silent.)*

You unfold a part of it, and there's this hinge, and a little bitty piece of the measurin' stick opens up. It's sections of a ruler, all hinged together like.

(more silence and more staring)

And then you unfold another part of it, and another little bitty piece of the stick opens up. You know them old–fashioned real long wooden rulers?

(more silence)

Little hinges? The wooden kind?

MOTHER. I'm lookin' at the sky here and I don't see me a single damn bird.

DADDY. That's how my body feels. Like an old wooden measurin' stick with hinges.

MOTHER. Where have all the damn birds gone to?

DADDY. Like an old wooden measurin' stick with hinges.

MOTHER. Means rain. Or some storm. When the birds go off somewhere and don't have the decency to tell anybody where they're goin'. I know the kind.

DADDY. You know the kind?

MOTHER. I said I did, didn't I? Yes. Yes.

DADDY. What?

MOTHER. What?

DADDY. What'd you say "yes" to? I didn't ask you nothin'.

MOTHER. You did too.

DADDY. I did?

MOTHER. You did.

DADDY. I asked you somethin'?

MOTHER. You asked me "the wooden kind".

DADDY. "The wooden kind". What the hell kind of question is that, "the wooden kind"? What are you talkin' about?

MOTHER. I'm talkin' about you're gettin' to be old. Real old. I'm talkin' about we're gonna have to put you in the Rubber Room down at Big Spring. *(looks out window)* Why don't I see me a single damn bird?

DADDY. I felt stiff is all I was sayin'. Like a creaky old measurin' stick openin' up in sections.

(He goes to refrigerator, takes out a pitcher and pours juice into a dirty glass he picks out of the sink.)

You want some juice?

MOTHER. No thank you. Lately it makes me gassy.

DADDY. It always did.

MOTHER. Did not.

DADDY. Did too. You remember when we were in the grocery store that time and you'd had juice that mornin' and you let out a big old economy size fart in the aisle next to the watermelons and nobody was around except for that little ugly kid with the ears and he started yellin' out "Yuck! Poo! Yuck! Poo!" You remember that?

(He thinks this is very funny.)

(long silence)

MOTHER. No. I can't say that I do.

DADDY. You don't remember "Yuck and poo"? The little ugly kid with the ears? Next to the watermelons?

MOTHER. I most certainly do not.

DADDY. Well, you see, that's your age talkin' right there. You're gettin' too old to recall details of things.

MOTHER. Memory loss is the best thing that ever happened to me.

DADDY. Why is that?

MOTHER. Saves time, saves effort. Tryin' to forget takes a hell of a lot of energy. Where are the damn birds?

DADDY. Tryin' to forget? What are you tryin' to forget?

MOTHER. I'm tryin' to forget I didn't do what I intended to do.

DADDY. What did you intend to do that you didn't do?

MOTHER. I intended to have children with an ounce or two of gratitude in their bones.

DADDY. Oh come on, Mother. Just settle yourself down now.

MOTHER. Don't you call me Mother. I'm not your mother. Your mother's dead and buried and roastin' in the hot flames of hell for all the mean things she ever did and said, every day of her shriveled up little meaningless life.

DADDY. Did you take your meds today?

MOTHER. I took my medicine, yes. Why do they call 'em meds anyway? 'Cause they don't have time to say the whole damn word?

DADDY. Mother, you seem testy today. You do.

MOTHER. 'Cause I got time. I got time to say the whole damn word. What else have I got to do with my time? Say the whole damn word.

DADDY. You do. You seem testy.

MOTHER. Here's what I'm thinkin', see. I'm thinkin' about time. What's left and how to spend it.

DADDY. I know.

MOTHER. Your mother wasn't nice.

DADDY. She wasn't.

MOTHER. We wasted a lot of time on that one.

DADDY. We did.

MOTHER. You could've saved a lot of time by just agreein' with me.

DADDY. Well, maybe so, but I was a little slow on that one.

MOTHER. A little slow? You think you were a little slow? I wish I had every minute back of the days and nights we spent discussin' that family nonsense. Me wantin' you to see my way of things, you needin' not to see it, back and forth and on and on, and tears and shouts and slammin' doors and wasted time, I tell you.

DADDY. I know.

MOTHER. It was our *life*. Our *time*. Our lifetime. That's how we spent it.

DADDY. I know.

MOTHER. Makes me want to just lie down and puke.

DADDY. Mother –

MOTHER. Don't call me…!

DADDY. Sorry.

(silence)

MOTHER. So what do you mean, you feel like an old-fashioned real long wooden measurin' stick with hinges? What the hell does that mean?

DADDY. I hurt. It hurts when I'm wakin' up. It hurts when I'm startin' to move around in the mornin'. Like I'm rusty. That's it. I'm rusty. It's hard to move. Hard to stand up. Hard to sit down. Hard to eat. Hard to pee. Hard to get places.

MOTHER. Hard to get places? Where the hell you goin'?

DADDY. Damned if I know.

(another silence)

MOTHER. Speakin' of goin', I still don't see me a single damn bird.

DADDY. You just don't let things go, do you? You're like a turtle bitin' on a finger. You're just gonna keep hangin' on it. Good Lord, woman.

MOTHER. And what happens when I don't see the birds is, I wonder why they've left. Do they know somethin'? You know. Like rats from a sinkin' ship?

DADDY. You always did worry too much.

MOTHER. I never could stop worryin'. Now I'm goin' to worry about you. I never knew you to complain before.

DADDY. I didn't complain. I just said I felt like a measurin' stick.

MOTHER. With rusty hinges. I'll say one thing for you though.

DADDY. What's that?

MOTHER. You're good humored.

DADDY. I'm good humored?

MOTHER. In the end, a good humor can balance out the wasted days and nights. A little bit.

DADDY. You think so?

MOTHER. Maybe.

DADDY. I'm good humored.

MOTHER. Mostly.

DADDY. Well thank you.

MOTHER. All right. *(long silence)* And the other thing.

DADDY. What other thing?

MOTHER. You know.

DADDY. What?

MOTHER. You know.

DADDY. What?

MOTHER. You know.

DADDY. Oh. That.

MOTHER. That was all right too.

DADDY. It was.

(another silence)

MOTHER. I'm lookin' at the sky here. Not one damn bird anywhere.

DADDY. Let me help.

(He joins her, standing behind her at the kitchen sink, his arms around her waist. They look out the window for a long time.)

MOTHER. You don't think the birds know somethin' we don't know? Some storm? Some bad thing comin'?

DADDY. You worry too much.

(They continue to stand looking out the window.)

SENSATIONS

CHARACTERS

MAN - 70, critical, cautious, judgmental
WOMAN - 70, chatty, light-hearted, trusting

*(A **MAN** and a **WOMAN**, both 70, seated in two chairs. They are in bath robes, but the robes are freshly laundered and crisply ironed, looking as if no one has spent a single moment sleeping in them. The **WOMAN** seems awake and alert and almost chatty, the **MAN** somewhat more subdued.)*

MAN. I'm remembering funny things now. Childhood things. Things that are obsolete. No longer useful. That's what I'm remembering.

WOMAN. Me, too. I was thinking of games. Jacks. Why would I be thinking of jacks? And have you noticed, the memories seem so tiny, like looking through the wrong end of binoculars? Everything's very clear, but quite small and far away. Is that the pills, do you think?

MAN. We had roller skates, the old kind with metal keys and that little worn leather strap that went over the toe of your shoe and held your foot in.

WOMAN. I loved those jacks. The metal points felt so good in your hand when you jumbled them up all together in a bunch.

MAN. I kept the skate key on a string around my neck.

WOMAN. And the little ball! So shiny! And sort of sticky and fire-engine red, but small, and with lots of bounce. Springy. Very hard to control.

MAN. Speaking of control, you do want to do this, right? Because if you don't, it's fine. It's just fine. You can say. We could call somebody. Dial 911?

WOMAN. Of course I want to do this. Of course! How can you doubt it?

MAN. It's all this talk about bunches of jacks or springy balls, or whatever.

WOMAN. I'm not talking. I'm reminiscing. We're reminiscing. That's different. Remember jump ropes?

MAN. What?

WOMAN. Jump ropes. They said it was why girls learned to read earlier than boys. All that early eye-hand coordination, you see. Running straight toward the jump rope, and then quick, once you were inside it and jumping, you had to start to say the rhyme and make it fit your rhythm. Amazing the skills we had to have for all that.

MAN. What are you talking about?

WOMAN. Focus. Concentration.

MAN. That's what you're talking about?

WOMAN. Yes. Focus. Concentration.

MAN. I'm not sure I believe this is reminiscing.

WOMAN. Excuse me?

MAN. I think it's nervous, babbling blather. And if you're nervous –

WOMAN. I'm not nervous.

MAN. But if.

WOMAN. I'm not nervous. No "if."

MAN. But just in case.

WOMAN. I'm not nervous. No "just in case." No "if."

MAN. All right.

WOMAN. I'm not.

MAN. All right. *(pause)* So now what. We wait?

WOMAN. We wait.

MAN. When does it start to take effect?

WOMAN. It's already started. It's taking.

MAN. Oh. And you checked everything one last time, right? Everything?

WOMAN. Good Lord. Of course I checked. What do you think I am? You never thought I could do anything. You never believed in my capabilities.

MAN. Don't be ridiculous. We're trying to get a job done here. We don't want to end up as eggplants. I have complete faith in you, I have total and absolute confidence in your capabilities. Tell me again, exactly how you proceeded.

WOMAN. I can't believe this. Isn't it a little late for this? I checked with Parker. To find out if I'd done it right. I was very subtle about it, too.

MAN. And?

WOMAN. Well, you know, Parker is understated.

MAN. Parker doesn't say much.

WOMAN. Not a lot of energy.

MAN. Pretty low key.

WOMAN. Not given to hyperbole.

MAN. No.

WOMAN. If the truth be known, Parker may not quite have understood what I was talking about.

MAN. Why do you say that?

WOMAN. Well, as I said before, I was very subtle. And her response was a little odd. All Parker said was, "Well, be careful."

MAN. "Well, be careful"?

WOMAN. Here's exactly how she said it. "Well, pause, be careful."

MAN. "Well, pause, be careful"? Be careful or what? We might die?

WOMAN. Honestly, I don't have a clue what Parker meant by it.

MAN. Parker has never been particularly helpful with anything. You ask her what day of the week it is, and she says she'll have to check with somebody and get back to you later. That's Parker.

WOMAN. Yes.

MAN. And still, Parker is the person whom you, in your infinite wisdom, chose to check with?

WOMAN. Here we go. Here it begins.

MAN. What a brilliant choice.

WOMAN. The little snide remarks that diminish the spirit.

MAN. You could have called the Red Cross. You could have gotten in touch with the Hemlock Society.

WOMAN. The derision. The erosion. The condescension.

MAN. Parker, upon hearing our plans, says, "Well, pause, be careful."

WOMAN. Parker did not *hear* our plans. I told you, I was very subtle. I said, "Sometimes we're extra careful about how we take our pills – so that they last."

MAN. That is not checking. That is not receiving information.

WOMAN. Wait a minute. Then I said, "Sometimes we don't take our medications the way we've been instructed to. We sort of save them, maybe for later, maybe for another time. Another time – when we might need them more." Then I added, "Do you think that's all right?"

MAN. Hence, the admonition: "Well, pause, be careful?"

WOMAN. Despite your unpleasant tone, you do have a point about Parker. So I went online.

MAN. You what?

WOMAN. That's right, Mr. Tell-Me-Again-Exactly-How-You-Proceeded. I went online. They showed me how to do it at the library. It's amazing what you can find on the information highway. I entered the word and all these things came up.

MAN. What word?

WOMAN. You know. Anyway, you'd be astonished. For example, somebody's selling a kit on the Internet, a plastic bag, along with the correct supply of pills. You take the pills, you slip the bag over your head and it does the rest. Except you won't endure any discomfort because by the time the bag is in the picture, so to speak, you're already out of the picture. Neat. Tidy. Tidy. Neat.

MAN. Did you order it?

WOMAN. It was too expensive.

MAN. What are you saving your money for, a Caribbean cruise?

WOMAN. You see, that's the tone right there. I say something simple. Direct. Unencumbered. You have to take a snippy little swipe at it.

MAN. Don't take everything so personally.

WOMAN. Ah, yes, man's response through the years to women who recognize the snippy little swipes for exactly what they are.

MAN. So. It's just the pills that we've saved up. Hoarded, as it were.

WOMAN. Just the pills.

MAN. That's it?

WOMAN. Just our saved up pills. No bag over the head. Simple is best.

MAN. And it's the right amount?

WOMAN. I certainly hope so. They were easy to swallow, weren't they?

MAN. Went down smooth as silk. *(long silence)* Here's the funny thing. When I think about my life? I don't remember anything except sensations.

WOMAN. Yes, sensations.

MAN. Sensations, very keenly recalled. Very colorful. Taste. Smell. Touch.

WOMAN. Yes and no. Keenly recalled and yet…

MAN. What?

WOMAN. It's not complete. You see, here's what I don't remember. Reasons for things. Why we fell in love. Why we moved to Chicago. Yet I remember pickles. I don't remember childbirth. I mean, I recall the fact of it. But I don't remember pain. I remember only how the babies smelled. Talcum and breath. I won't be breathing. How strange that will seem.

MAN. You remember pickles?

WOMAN. And all those things we battled over? Who was right, who was wrong, who didn't speak, who wouldn't apologize, who had to make a point, who didn't want to listen. All those things, I don't remember any more.

MAN. You remember pickles?

WOMAN. So clearly. A pickle took your lip and sucked on it. Hard. You thought what you were doing was sucking on *it*. No. It was sucking on *you*. It had the pull of a lover's bite on your mouth.

(silence)

MAN. That's very erotic.

WOMAN. You think so?

MAN. Yes.

WOMAN. You know what it's going to be like? It's going to be like swimming. That's all. Exactly like swimming. Which, now that I think of it, is a little frightening. Yes, I always thought swimming was a little frightening. Like being a baby floating around in your mother's womb. Not knowing which end is up. Or when you're going to get out. So yes, I believe that's how it's going to be.

MAN. That thing you said about the pickles? I'm still thinking about it.

WOMAN. Yes?

MAN. And you know something? You still seem unusually chatty to me. Are you sure about these pills? I mean what if all they make you do is talk a lot, instead of, you know, doing the trick?

WOMAN. The trick?

MAN. You are talking a great deal. We haven't talked like this in years. And all that stuff about being a baby floating around in your mother's womb, not knowing which end is up? Or when you're going to get out? You know something? You're stoned.

WOMAN. Really?

MAN. Absolutely.

WOMAN. You think?

MAN. I'm certain.

WOMAN. But it's such a nice sensation. It's not death?

MAN. I told you. Stoned. And that thing about the pickle? Wonderful stuff!

WOMAN. What should we do? Should we call someone?

MAN. Who would we call?

WOMAN. We could call Parker.

MAN. What would Parker do? Nothing.

WOMAN. Maybe doing nothing has its own rewards.

MAN. Maybe so. I mean, look at this, look at us. Our plan doesn't seem to be working. Isn't that wonderful?

WOMAN. To tell you the truth, I've been a little nervous about it.

MAN. Really?

WOMAN. Yes. Will we be all right? I can't remember anymore why we were doing this.

MAN. Reasons for things. As you said, they fade like wisps of clouds. Just keep talking. All we have is sensations, remember? Something will wind down eventually. Either the pills or us. Then we'll sleep.

WOMAN. Later we'll sleep. Hold my hand.

MAN. I will.

(They hold hands as the lights fade.)

THE RIVER JORDAN LAMP

CHARACTERS

WOMAN - 45-50, simple, countrywoman, a little worn by a hardscrabble life, living alone in her trailer

(A simple country **WOMAN***…a little worn by a hardscrabble life. She is sweeping inside the trailer that is her home.)*

WOMAN. I reckon that lamp was just about the nicest thing I ever owned. I'll bet even Liberace never had anything that pretty. You know I'm tellin' the truth, Lord. You know that!

(More sweeping. Then she stops, leans on the broom.)

'Cause what it was, see, was a color photograph of the River Jordan, printed right onto the lamp shade. And there was somethin' inside the lamp, so that when the bulb was lit up, the River Jordan looked like it was flowin'.

(Lights come up a little.)

That's right! Praise God! Movin' along, like a real river, with the hills of the Holy Land all lit up behind it, like the sun was shinin'. And down at the bottom of the lamp? Well, I still don't know how they done it, but it was carved like a statue, and would you believe, it was the Last Supper? *All* of it! Every last one of 'em. Jesus and the Twelve Disciples, and the table and the bread and the wine, and even a little clump of grapes on a dish, all formed out of this real pretty pink colored plaster of Paris. Thank you, Lord, for givin' me the mind to notice my blessings. I never saw anything so beautiful in my life.

(She puts the broom away and sits down.)

I used to sit here in the trailer late at night with all the lights turned off except for my River Jordan lamp. And no matter how lonesome I was feelin', I'd get me a cool glass of buttermilk, I'd sit here awhile, and the peace that passeth all understanding would just roll right on over me, 'til I finally got sleepy and could snap off that bulb.

WOMAN. *(cont.)* Every night I would just sit in the dark and watch that River flow.

(She gets up, goes to the sink, fills a kettle with water, and puts it on the stove to boil. Then she returns to her chair.)

Lookin' back on it now, there ain't nobody to blame but my own self. You and I both know that's the truth. I practically thumbed a ride up the path to Fool's Hill. It's late one summer afternoon, and I hear a knock at the trailer door, and I go to answer and there's this Mexican kid. About seventeen. Skinny as a bean, and the biggest brown eyes you ever saw. Quite a smile on him, though. He says he don't want nothin' but work, and do I need a yard boy? He's good at weedin', he says. Well, you know I always have been a sucker for kids, ever since my baby sister passed on. And if a kid's willin' to work, that means they ain't on the dole, and I like that. So before I know it, Ramon's in my yard, weedin'.

That's his name, Ramon. Pretty name. Fits his smile.

*(The tea kettle starts to bubble now, and the **WOMAN** goes to the stove and pours the water into an old cracked tea cup. She takes a sip.)*

Later in the afternoon he's out in the squash bed, and I bring him some iced tea and an old cold biscuit, and do you know, he offers to pay me for 'em! Oh boy, I'm a goner after that one. So at the end of the afternoon I tell him he can come back another time later on, to fix my leaky faucet.

Ramon's big old brown eyes fill up then, and he says he's gonna do a novena for me or some such thing they do over at the Roman Church. I tell him just come back and fix the leaky faucet. All that pagan stuff makes me jumpy.

That night I'm sittin' in front of the River Jordan lamp, and I'll tell you the truth, Lord, I'm kinda lookin' forward to havin' some company.

*(Lights change to slightly brighter tone. The **WOMAN** begins to move about the trailer, arranging cans on a shelf, wiping Mason jars, cleaning a cast iron skillet with some dry cornmeal.)*

Ramon comes back a few days later to fix the faucet, and he does a real fine job, so it seems like a good idea to let him start cleanin' out the tool shed. I mean, what with my bein' alone and all, there's some heavy work I haven't gotten to yet, and now that I have help handy, it's easy to think of things. The pick-up needs Simonizin', I got some scrap iron to haul, stuff needs paintin', that kind of thing. I give him half a dollar and a sandwich for it every time.

And Ramon's a real good worker. He's comin' almost every day now, and I tell you, I'm keepin' him busier than a long-tailed cat in a roomful o' rockers. We visit a little sometimes, and I can see he's got spunk. He tells me his daddy's pickin' peaches, his mama's run off somewhere, he's got six little brothers and sisters. But he wants to improve himself. Go to school and such. Maybe get a job in town some day.

That's how I come to teach him to drive the pick-up. I figure maybe that could help him get a town job.

And oh boy, does Ramon love drivin'! That first day, when I offer to show him how, his face lights up like the River Jordan lamp itself, and it don't take long before we're bumpin' along the back road, lettin' out the clutch and laughin', and lettin' out the clutch and laughin', and lettin' out the clutch and laughin', and after he finally gets it smooth and he's drivin' good now, well, Ramon starts singin'. And he's singin' all the way out to the end of Lemon Gap Road. Comin' back he teaches me the song, too. Me! I'm singin' in Mexican! And, Lord, his drivin's makin' me laugh, and my singin's makin' him laugh, and we surely do have ourselves a high old time that afternoon, I tell you. We surely do.

(She sits.)

WOMAN. *(cont.)* That night, I sit in front of the lamp and sing for hours. I make a joyful noise unto you, Lord! I figure, Jesus and the Disciples probably enjoys Mexican songs, too.

(Lights change, become softer.)

What happens next is a little hard to recall exactly. All I remember is, it's a time when all the squash is put up, and the tool shed's clean as a whistle, and it's gettin' long past the end of summer. I do recollect, too, now that I think on it, that I'd been havin' a chill in my bones.

I figure it's the change in the weather.

One evenin' around suppertime, I'm paintin' an old chifforobe in the yard, and I see Ramon walkin' up the road to the trailer like he does every day, but this time that smile of his is wiped right off his face, and his big old eyes are lookin' wide. Serious.

He says his daddy's told him they have to head north now to pick apples. Right away. Tonight. Ramon's gotta go with him, to take care of the brothers and sisters. With the little bit of money he's made from bein' my yard man all summer, and with the fact he can drive now, his daddy says Ramon's doin' better than any of 'em. They need him, of course. He's got to go.

(She stands up, goes to a small pile of clean laundry, and begins to fold it.)

Well, I don't know why I feel so surprised, Lord. It's not like Ramon and me ever talked about it, one way or the other, stayin' or goin'. We were always just planted where we were then, if you follow me.

(She leans against the sink.)

I feel funny all of a sudden. Maybe it's the cool wind comin' in off the ridge. I tell Ramon I got to sit down in a soft chair.

So I open the screen door of the trailer to go inside, and Ramon follows me in, to make sure I'm all right.

I remember thinkin' it was probably unusual, us bein' friends and all, that Ramon had never been in my little trailer house until that very minute.

(She sits down.)

I sit down in my soft chair, and Ramon goes to get me a cup of water. That's when he sees my River Jordan lamp.

Well, he just goes completely silly. He's like some fool, carryin' on, jumpin' around to see it from all different sides. He turns the light on and off about a hundred times so he can watch the River stop and go and stop and go. I say Ramon, you're makin' me nervous, but he's payin' me no mind. And now he's bendin' and bowin' in front of it, makin' the sign of the cross or some crazy thing, and I'm sayin' Ramon, stop that foreign idol-worship, this is a house of Jesus! But, you know, while I'm sayin' it, we're both of us startin' to smile.

Then Ramon does a real funny thing. He gets quiet. He comes over to me and kneels. Kneels! I'm sittin' in my chair, and he puts his head right on my knee. He wraps those skinny bean arms around me, and he looks up with those big old eyes, and he says he wants me to give him somethin' to remember our friendship by. Anything at all. He says nobody but me was ever his friend, and he'll never forget it. But he wants somethin' to carry with him.

Well. There we are. Ramon and me. This fool Mexican kid wrappin' his arms around my…well, now it's my waist, I guess. Yes. By now his arms are around my waist and his head is sort of on my lap, and I guess you'd say he's cryin', and to tell you the truth, so am I.

I think about how nobody ever gave him nothin', and nobody ever gave me nothin', and now we're both cryin', and the River Jordan is flowin', and Lord, I ask you what to do then. I do. And I can't hear the answer.

WOMAN. *(cont.)* I can't hear anything except Ramon and me cryin' together.

Ramon's hair is real smooth. I never touched Mexican hair before. And those skinny bean arms? Well, who would've thought he'd know so much about what we did? Lord have mercy. Anyway, I snap off the lamp. It's commencin' to get dark outside but I can see Ramon's smile in the shadows.

(a moment of silence)

I guess you could say I give him something to remember our friendship by.

(another moment)

And I'll tell you the truth, that's not the part I regret. The part I regret is, afterwards, while I'm takin' a nap, that little greaser stole my lamp.

The way I figure it, Lord, that's your way of punishin' me for my sin of the flesh. Funny thing. I don't feel bad about givin' him the yard work or teachin' him to drive or any of the rest of it.

But I tell you, I sure am gonna miss watchin' that River Jordan flow.

(The lights dim very slowly. Our last view is her face.)

It's just so dark where I am.

JACK AND JILL

CHARACTERS

JACK - 40, brother, calm, even-tempered, the person everyone else depends on

JILL - 40, sister, permanently upset

(**JACK** *and* **JILL**, *in their forties. They are brother and sister.*)

(*At opening,* **JILL** *seems visibly upset.* **JACK** *is calm.*)

JILL. I can't believe it.

JACK. Me either.

JILL. I just can't believe it.

JACK. I know. Me either.

JILL. Do you understand what I'm saying? I'm saying I. CAN. NOT. BELIEVE. IT.

JACK. I'm with you all the way on this, yes, no, I understand, all right? Me either.

JILL. Actually, that's wrong. The words "can not" are wrong. The words "can not" imply an inability of some sort. "Will not" is what I mean. "I will not" as in "I refuse," as in "I decline to accept," as in "I reject." I reject it. I will not believe it.

JACK. Yes, I understand.

JILL. This changes everything.

JACK. Okay. Yes.

JILL. Virtually our entire lives.

JACK. I know.

JILL. Nothing will ever be as it was.

JACK. Absolutely. All right.

JILL. After all this time?

JACK. Long time.

JILL. Thirty-five years?

JACK. I don't know. It seems forever. Long time.

JILL. What do they give as their reason?

JACK. They don't.

JILL. They give no reason? No reason whatsoever?

JACK. Nope.

JILL. From whence cometh their blinding new insight?

JACK. Got me.

JILL. As if it mattered. As if they cared. We're only the children. *Their* children. The "adult children". And by the way, what kind of wooly muffle oxymoronic phrase is *that* to describe us?

JACK. Oxymoronic?

JILL. An oxymoron is a figure of speech that combines contradictory terms…like jumbo shrimp?

JACK. Adult children.

JILL. Yes. But I digress. We are the children, the issue of their loins, now grown into maturity. That's us. But what weight does *that* carry in the great cosmic scheme of totally meaningless verbiage used to describe a family?

JACK. You're upset.

JILL. I'm not upset.

JACK. You seem upset.

JILL. I don't seem upset. I seem curious. Curious is what I seem. Puzzled. Full of questions. Tell me again: what do they give as their reason?

JACK. They've come to this decision after much thoughtful consideration.

JILL. What about the years of therapy?

JACK. They didn't mention the years of therapy.

JILL. No, I guess not, I guess they didn't mention the years of therapy. Getting us used to the way it was.

JACK. They say they're more mature now.

JILL. More mature? They call it mature that after thirty-five years of divorce – a worked through, planned out, analyzed *ad nauseam*, perfectly ordinary, average, middle class American divorce – they have decided to go back together to live as man and wife again, happily ever after, under one roof? They call that mature?

JACK. They've fallen back in love.

JILL. Don't be ridiculous!

JACK. They've found one another again.

JILL. Oh, please. Give me a break.

JACK. They're wiser. This is what they said.

JILL. They're not wiser, they're just old. What about us? WHAT ABOUT THE YEARS OF THERAPY?

JACK. They know more what they want out of life.

JILL. Years of therapy. Hostility! Guilt! Accept this! Express that!

JACK. They say certain things seem more important to them now. Or is it certain things seem less important to them now?

JILL. Years of therapy! Leather couches. Beige walls. Boxes of tissues.

JACK. They hope we'll support them in this decision.

JILL. How can they do this to us? We understood everything. It was all worked out.

JACK. They say it won't be that different, really.

JILL. It will be completely different! What about the holidays? The holidays will be totally destroyed. In shreds. Christmas will be a train wreck. Passover, forget about it, why even bother? Mother's Day! Father's Day! Remember those? My God!

JACK. Listen to me.

JILL. In shreds!

JACK. Listen to me.

JILL. We were used to the way it was.

JACK. Listen to me.

JILL. No! What?

JACK. We have to accept it.

JILL. Why? Why do we have to accept it?

JACK. For the same reason we accepted all the rest.

JILL. And that is?

JACK. We can't prevent it. They're going back together.

JILL. How can they? How dare they? Thirty-five years.

JACK. We can't stop them.
JILL. In shreds.
JACK. We have each other.
JILL. It was all such a waste.
JACK. Yes, it was. *(He reaches for her hand.)* We have each other.

(They sit for a long moment.)

JILL. Yes. So here we are. Alone together. That's us.
JACK. Yes. Alone together.
JILL. That's us.
JACK. Alone together. Oxymoron?
JILL. Yes.
JACK. Yes.

(lights fade)

THE DAYS ARE AS GRASS

CHARACTERS

WOMAN - 60-65, quick, bright, wise, centered

MAN - 40-45, attractive, literate, intelligent, sardonic

(A beautiful restaurant. An elegant **WOMAN** *about sixty, sits alone, utterly comfortable with herself, with where she is, and with waiting. She holds a lavender colored cigarette in a long black holder, looks about the room, sips a glass of wine.)*

(A **MAN**, *handsome, well-dressed, forty-something, approaches the table.)*

MAN. If anyone had told me that twenty years later you'd still be smoking those ridiculous lavender cigarettes, I would have said they were crazy. Can you still buy the bright pink ones?

WOMAN. You can still buy the bright pink ones. I wonder who does. Actually, I gave up smoking a long time ago. This was just a clue for you, so that after twenty years you could still find me in a crowded room. *(She opens her arms to give him an embrace.)*

MAN. No one ever had a problem finding you in a crowded room.

(He gives her a big friendly hug. They smile at one another.)

You really do look exactly the same.

WOMAN. One of the things I always liked about you was that you had no natural charm whatsoever. Please don't disappoint me now.

MAN. I mean it. Exactly the same. From the hair to the twinkle in the eyes.

WOMAN. I'm going to fling my body in front of a moving train if I have to, to make you stop this.

MAN. *(sitting)* I can't help it if you're still beautiful.

WOMAN. I look all right, but basically, we're talking an old ruin in the moonlight. Do you know what I mean? Do you want wine?

MAN. No, I've got cranberry juice here. Less sodium. For salt retention.

WOMAN. Salt retention?

MAN. Puffiness. The camera.

WOMAN. Oh certainly. I should have thought of that myself. Puffiness. The camera.

MAN. No face lift then?

WOMAN. Excuse me?

MAN. Old ruin in the moonlight. No face lift?

WOMAN. Me? You can't be serious. The very idea of it is awful. Pay good money so somebody can snip away at the skin of your face? Pull it up and around, and this way and that, and then sew it all back together like old slipcovers being altered for a new couch? Certainly not. I'm much too vain to have a face lift. I don't want to talk about me. Come on, tell me everything about cranberry juice and the camera and what it's like being a movie star. That's what you are. You've done everything you used to say you were going to do. Are you happy? You look well.

MAN. Am I happy? A little more cranberry juice before we get to that one. What do you mean, I look "well"? It sounds awful.

WOMAN. I mean good. I mean healthy. I mean, as a young man you were beautiful and now its all turning very nicely into character. You look invigorated.

MAN. I don't think I can stand much more. Invigorated? Screw you.

WOMAN. Are you being funny or do you mean this? Oh my. You mean this. Oh all right, here's a rave review. You have single-handedly defeated salt retention. There now. Is this what its like talking to a movie star? I never did before.

MAN. I'm not a movie star. I'm a working actor. I always seem to play the sardonic best friend or the weird neighbor with the dead body hidden in the basement. I was once nominated for a Golden Globe for Best

Supporting Actor but I didn't win. This week I came close to, but did not get, an opportunity to be the spokesperson of a national TV campaign. According to my agent, I was described, and I quote, as being "just a little light in the loafers for the Bank of America."

WOMAN. Light in the loafers?

MAN. By which, I presume, they mean I am minutes away from playing the prissy Vicar in an Agatha Christie mini-series. I just finished paying for my second eye lift, and you think I look "invigorated", I have not done everything I said I would do, and after twenty years your first question to me is am I happy? Tell me the truth, have you ever met anyone forty years old who was happy?

WOMAN. Do you know what my favorite thing about you always was?

MAN. You already said. No natural charm whatsoever.

WOMAN. No. I said that was one of the things I liked. My *favorite* was that you were the only person I've ever met who could quote from anything you'd read. No matter who it was, Shakespeare, Tennyson, Oscar Wilde, Bob Dylan, Piglet…you'd say something on the order of "'We think in generalities, but we live in details' - Alfred North Whitehead!" I was so impressed. It was all I could do to manage "As God is my witness, I'll never go hungry again." So, what are you reading? Today? Right now?

MAN. All right, I'll play this familiar little game. But don't think I don't know what you're doing. That question "Are you happy?" is going to rise from its ashes. My reading this week has been eclectic, to say the least. I started with Virginia Wolfe (The novel written right before she drowned herself in the river). Then I took a little detour into Sylvia Plath's work. Wasn't it kind of awful the way she put her head in the oven while her two little children were still in the house? And after that I couldn't even get through Ezra Pound's poems, the ones he wrote while he was institutionalized. From there, I just headed straight for *People Magazine*. I like the issue about the Fifty Most Beautiful People In the World.

WOMAN. That's not a bit funny.

MAN. What's not funny?

WOMAN. Depression. Sadness. You.

MAN. I don't read anymore.

(There is a pause while she looks carefully at him.)

WOMAN. You don't read anymore?

MAN. Everything is different now.

(Another silence. She is still looking at him.)

I gave up reading when the Russians began to make sense.

WOMAN. The Russians?

MAN. Dostoyevsky. *The Brothers Karamazov.* Remember the thing he says about hell?

WOMAN. Is that "Hell is other people"?

MAN. I'm ashamed of you. That's Sartre, that's from *No Exit*, and you really ought to know better. This is Dostoyevsky: "I ponder what is hell. I maintain it is the suffering of being unable to love."

WOMAN. Ridiculous. Hell is the suffering of being *able* to love. Dostoyevsky can't see that?

MAN. "Dostoyevsky can't see that?" I'll say one thing for you. You always thought your opinions were equal to anybody's. You'd argue your way past St. Peter at the Gate, if you had to.

WOMAN. So hell is the suffering of being unable to love, you don't read anymore, and everything is different now?

MAN. Right.

WOMAN. Is this a good time to tell you that I still love you?

MAN. No. It's not. As a matter of fact, it would probably depress me.

WOMAN. I still love you.

MAN. Sensitive as ever to other people's needs, I see.

WOMAN. Why would that depress you?

MAN. Nothing personal. It just reminds me that so much time has passed. By the way, are you still married to that man?

WOMAN. No. I am no longer married to that man or to one who came after him. Being married is sort of like having a green thumb or perfect pitch. It's a talent. You either have it or you don't. I didn't. I was married three times and the trouble was that every single time my husband and I would end up falling deeply in love with the same person.

MAN. Who?

WOMAN. Me. I couldn't help myself. I always thought I was a little more interesting than they were.

MAN. Oh, you were interesting, all right.

WOMAN. Why is everything different now? Why aren't you happy?

MAN. You were interesting in the sense that it's interesting being run over by a tank. You required blood, guts, tears, sweat, phone calls, letters, visits, secrets, time, undying devotion, and a weekly book report from everyone you ever met.

WOMAN. That's not true. You were the only person I ever shared books with. With us it was no flimsy matter of the heart. We had an affair of the mind! We fed one another: novels, poetry, ideas, literary quotes…like we were popping chocolates in each other's mouths. Do you remember when I called you at two in the morning because I had just discovered Rilke?

MAN. Rilke: "Love consists in this: that two souls border and protect and greet one another." I also remember what I was doing and who I was doing it with when you called at two in the morning. I can assure you, no one I ever met understood our friendship. Least of all you and me.

WOMAN. Is that why you left me? Because you didn't understand our friendship? Or because you did? Because I wasn't the one with you at two in the morning? Or because that's what we both wanted and you didn't know what to do about it? I called you to come have a drink with me tonight because I want to know why you left me.

MAN. I never left you. I wasn't with you. You just said it was an affair of the mind.

WOMAN. I don't understand. That nullifies its strength? The mind is less important than the crotch? The brain is weaker than the genitalia?

MAN. You mean you never noticed that?

WOMAN. *You were, too, with me.*

MAN. Was not.

WOMAN. Were.

MAN. Was not.

WOMAN. Were.

MAN. Was not!

WOMAN. All right. For the moment. Have it your own way. My turn now. I still don't understand why you don't read anymore. Books were the glue that held you together. You loved them so! You used to talk about them with such understanding and excitement and affection – the story, the characters, the lyricism of a phrase, the music of a noun – and every once in a while, it would feel as if you'd taken on one special book as your new lover. You'd be introducing it to the world with joy and pride. We'd have to take it out to dinner and talk to it all evening. You'd carry two or three books around with you all the time, and if you had a rare old leather-bound one, you'd rub the soft cover very gently and put your face up to it and croon, "Smell this! Breath this in!" You'd loan me a book, and demand that I read it immediately, and then later that evening you'd phone up and say, "Okay, where are you?" And I'd answer with something like, "They just said goodbye at the train station," or "He's killing the lion," and you'd shout, "Hurry, you're almost to the best part." Your passion set me on fire. It set me on fire.

(There is a long silence. He looks at her.)

MAN. Reading didn't actually help anything. It just used to make me less lonely.

WOMAN. Less lonely?

MAN. You'll recall that I never could stand silence. Reading filled the space and took up time. Yes, less lonely. And speaking of lonely, you'll be pleased to know that I think maybe I'm coming to the "happy" question. I mean, the question you asked was "am I", and the answer is "no, I'm not."

WOMAN. Why?

MAN. Why? Well. *(counts the words on his fingers)* There was love. Now there's not. He was here. Now he's left. There it is. See, I've just summed it all up in fifteen one-syllable words. Isn't that interesting? Aren't words fascinating? The story is ordinary. After twelve years, the love of my life left me. For a twenty-three year-old. Wait a minute, did I say that correctly? Should I have said he left me, *with* a twenty-three year-old? No, all wrong. He left *me*, with the apartment and the two cats. I never was any good with prepositional phrases and their objects. Are they the ones that dangle? No, that's participles.

WOMAN. Stop it. Go on with the story.

MAN. Stop. Go. Go. Stop. Here it is. He chose to leave me *for*, and accompanied *by*, his friend, the twenty-three year-old. That's it. Wouldn't you call that a cliché? Did I say that or is it a lyric? Anyway, after that, I fell into a sort of slough of despair, or what I've come to call The Great Cosmic Why Bother. That's when you walk along the street on a beautiful Spring day and you look up at the sky and see that the pretty puffy clouds have suddenly formed themselves into alphabet letters that spell out the question "Why bother?" The same thing happens with a neon sign outside a café; you pass by it, the sign flashes "Open – Open – Open." Moments later it's flashing "why – bother – why – bother – why – bother." Then there are formations of geese that...

WOMAN. Stop being brittle. Will you please just tell me what happened?

MAN. This twenty-three year-old, by the way, is not only beautiful, ambitious, and talented, he is...and this part is almost funny...a personal trainer who has an MA in Dramaturgy from Yale. Amazing, huh? Yale. Dramaturgy. A personal trainer. I have an awful feeling I sound like a bitchy old queen. What the hell is Dramaturgy anyway?

WOMAN. Go on.

MAN. Because if I do sound like a bitchy old queen, it's only because, as you would say, I...still...love him... *(He stops.)*

WOMAN. For God's sake, will you have something to drink besides cranberry juice?

MAN. Do you know, I actually used to read aloud to the two of them while they did their sit-ups? I should get an award. Something special, given to the person slowest to catch on to what's happening...a big heavy Golden Snail, perhaps?

WOMAN. Listen to me. You're concentrating on the wrong part of the story. The twenty-three year old isn't the important thing? He almost doesn't matter.

MAN. Doesn't matter? What do you mean?

WOMAN. It's stressful to be a twenty-three year old. They have no clear idea of themselves, and then of course there are those hormones. The twenty-three year old is bound to run into the force of gale winds he hadn't expected. Life will etch itself upon him. It's inevitable. He will move on, I can almost promise you that. But he's not your concern. Your beloved, now, *there's* the thing to be worked out. It's not the running away that's the hard part, it's the coming back. You. How angry are you? How angry will you stay? How quickly can you forgive? *Should* you forgive? What's in it for you if you do? If you don't? These are real questions worth debating. You might consider reading Robert Frost.

MAN. You think he will come back?

WOMAN. I can't say. But he doesn't have to be here for you to forgive him, does he?

MAN. "It's not the running away that's the hard part, it's the coming back?" I can't tell if you're trying to be The Delphic Sybil or Glenda the Good Witch.

WOMAN. I'm attempting wisdom here.

MAN. Maybe you're just being didactic.

WOMAN. Maybe I just like to tie up loose ends. Maybe I miss you and me. And if I may speak frankly, I don't think you're in Dostoyevsky's hell because you're unable to love. You're just furious and in pain and terrified.

MAN. That pretty much sums it up.

WOMAN But don't you see, that's the part that connects you to everyone else. That's the part the books were always about. I think the reason you're not reading is because you don't *want* to be less lonely. You like it here, slopping around in the great Cosmic Why Bother. Anyway, yes, I'm attempting wisdom. Pounded out and melted down and poured from the crucible of missed connections, fumbling mistakes and lost friends. Like us.

MAN. We weren't lost.

WOMAN. No?

MAN. No.

WOMAN. No?

MAN. Yes.

WOMAN. Do you remember the last time we spoke? You indicated, I believe, that I was requiring too much of you.

MAN. *(with a smile)* No one could read that much.

WOMAN. Something about intensity?

MAN. You have to admit, it was intense.

WOMAN. I never did learn to love without being, as you put it, intense. I always felt as if I were in one of those hotel showers where you can't find the medium temperature on the water, only the scalding hot or the icy cold.

MAN. "Neither abstinence nor excess ever renders Man happy." Voltaire.

WOMAN. "Neither abstinence nor excess ever renders man happy." Why does that make me think of eating ice cream? What you said was, you could no longer be my friend. You had a desire for distance. I see now that this was an odd request for a man who can't stand silence and needs to fill up space and time. But you see, for me, what had been happening between us was life-giving. Our minds, the books, the energy, the life, the laughter, had been replenishing. You had been like breath, you had sustained me. That's because I was almost forty then, and feeling much closer to the end than to the beginning.

MAN. Closer to the end than to the beginning. Oh, yes.

WOMAN. It can make one tremble. Go shaky in the knees.

MAN. Shaky. Tremble. Yes.

WOMAN. Therefore, losing you hurt. I cried. I lay on beds and walked in parks and stayed up nights, weeping till I was sopping. I grieved for the loss of someone to call in the middle of the night about a poem. I held you in my heart like a meditation. I read James Joyce and understood him. That was alarming. I felt old. Everything was difficult. Finally I took to thinking of myself in terms of cheese.

MAN. What do you mean, cheese?

WOMAN. I decided my melancholy required careful and proper aging. Chekhov helped.

MAN. And now?

WOMAN. That's what I'm trying to tell you about the coming back. I feel much closer to the beginning now than to the end. Isn't that odd? Old age is a place of fierce energy. There's a kind of passion you only get at the end of your life. Perhaps it is always there, but when you're twenty, you're too young to experience it.

MAN. And when you're forty?

WOMAN. That's a good time to figure out the forgiving. It takes a while. But it's worth it. It's worth it. This is the good news I'm bringing you, from my place out here on the edge of mortality. Don't give up the books! Don't give up what makes you feel less lonely. Don't give up the fire.

MAN. About us. It all terrified me.

WOMAN. Of course it did. You were very young. You didn't want to replenish anybody.

MAN. I needed only the lightest and gentlest touch.

WOMAN. Yes, you were a baby. You couldn't sustain a soul.

MAN. You made me nervous.

WOMAN. Absolutely. Understandable.

MAN. I couldn't be with you anymore.

WOMAN. Oh, were you with me?

(a moment)

MAN. Was. Yes.

WOMAN. Was. Yes.

MAN. Yes, and then I left you.

WOMAN. But here we are. You've come back.

MAN. Have I?

WOMAN. Yes. And so might your friend.

MAN. You think love can survive?

WOMAN. It's entirely possible. But even better, I think you will survive love.

MAN. It won't take twenty years?

WOMAN. Maybe not. Things seem to be moving along much faster these days.

MAN. I don't even know why I bother asking. I've never dealt very well with silence, space, distance *or* time.

WOMAN. Oh, well, who does, really? But reading does help. Knowing Dostoyevsky may have had a rough time is very comforting.

MAN. Do you remember this? "As for man, his days are as grass…"

WOMAN. "A flower of the field, he flourishes…"

MAN. "The wind passes over, it is gone…"

WOMAN. "And the place shall know it no more." What does that have to do with Dostoyevsky?

MAN. What do you mean? Dostoyevsky wrote it.

WOMAN. He did not. That's the one hundred and third psalm.

MAN. Are you crazy? I'm sure it's some Russian. Tolstoy, that's all I'll give you…

WOMAN. I can't believe you've gotten this rusty on details. "Some Russian?" You're illiterate! Too much cranberry juice. Not enough sodium in your system.

MAN. It's entirely possible that your age has actually affected your memory.

WOMAN. Waiter! A double vodka martini please!

MAN. Make that two…

WOMAN. It *was* the one hundred and third psalm…

MAN. Was not…

WOMAN. Was!

MAN. Was not…

WOMAN. Was!

MAN. Was not…

WOMAN. Was!

(They are arguing happily as the curtain comes down.)

THE LAST WORD

CHARACTERS

WOMAN - 50+, in a wheelchair, paralyzed but full of thoughts

MAN - 50+, optimistic, kind, always hoping for the best

*(A **WOMAN** sits in a wheel chair as a **MAN** pushes it slowly down the sidewalk. She is incapacitated and, although he is cheerfully talkative, she does not appear to be able to respond, so we are not sure how much she understands. Her body is immobilized – not in a way that's "stiff" – more a matter of arms and legs being weak. He points out items in store windows and talks to her about them, as if she is capable of understanding him perfectly. They move down the street toward a bus stop and a bench.)*

MAN. Here we go. There you are. Let's come over here and look at these. I know you like to look at colorful things. See those little dresses there? Aren't they colorful? They're very pretty, aren't they? Fluffy. Pretty, fluffy, little dresses. I recall when you wore dresses like that. I do! You looked like a little cloud when you came into the room. You did! Like a little, billowing cloud.

*(The **WOMAN** does not respond.)*

Would our granddaughter wear something like that, do you think? I don't think so, her having that tattoo of the snake on her neck. It wouldn't go well with the fluffy dresses, would it? I think not. No. I remember when a tattoo was something a sailor might get if he was drunk in a bar in Bangkok. Now they've got tattoos on people in nice magazines and on TV and everything. And on our granddaughter's neck.

You finished looking at those dresses? The bus should be here soon. We've got another minute. Let's go over here and see the shoes. Now, how do you girls get around in those little spindly shoes?

(He squints into the window.)

I never did know how you put those things on, much less how you walk around in them or move fast or go dancing. We sure went dancing, didn't we? Didn't we go dancing? Do you remember what you first tried to teach me? You tried to teach me to do the waltz! That's right – the waltz – and you didn't merely attempt it – you succeeded! I learned! I remember what you told me. You said, "It's just three little steps. Any fool can do three little steps. *One*-two-three. *One*-two-three."

(He gently lifts her arm, takes one of her hands in his hand, and, standing beside her chair, does a few small dance steps in place, all the while counting to himself.)

One-two-three, *one*-two-three, *one*-two-three...

(The woman does not react to him. After a few moments, he stops and carefully places her hand back in her lap. He looks at her for a long time.)

We'll just wait for the bus here. We'll just wait.

(At the bus stop, He pushes the chair next to the bench, locks the wheels and sits down.)

I wish I knew if you could understand me. I wish I knew. But if you can't, if you can't understand me, I think that's a good thing. I do. Because God knows, if you could understand me, you would want to reply. "Reply" is hardly the word. You would want to engage me in vigorous conversation. You would want to tell me about your day or pass on some news you picked up at the dry cleaners or argue about politics. That's what you'd want. You would not want to be sitting there in silence. In your prison of silence. You would not want that.

(silence)

You know, I always thought, if I had ever been tempted to be unfaithful to you – I always thought I would've had to find a really dull, boring woman to do it with. Because, after all my years with you, I just wouldn't have had the pep for anything else.

(He laughs. He thinks this is funny.)

I only mean because you were bright and sparkly, full of chatter, lots of conversation, many thoughts on many subjects – I always said, you could talk thirty minutes to the wrong number.

(silence)

Do you recall that night you threw the jar of prickly pear jelly at me? That was something, wasn't it? What were we arguing about, I wonder, do you remember? Now, why am I asking you that? What do I think I'm doing, asking you that? I think you were really mad at me about…I don't know…seems like it might have been about my brother. Was it about my brother? Well. My brother. What can I say? That man has spent his whole life being in love with the last word. He has to have that last word! He lusts after that last word. He'll give up anything for it – marriage, friends, job – they all pale in the face of his devotion to having the last word. And apologize? Doesn't know the meaning of it. That man wouldn't apologize if apologizing would bring peace to the Middle East. So, where was I? Oh, yes. So it was probably about my brother, and you were probably right to throw the prickly pear jelly. Is it too late to tell you that? I think it is. I think it's too late to tell you.

(silence)

What am I doing here? Rambling on like this. Drivel. Let's just sit for a while. Let's just both sit in silence here for a while.

(silence)

Sometimes silence is nice, isn't it? It can be nice.

(silence)

I like silence. I do.

(silence)

You remember the day we got married? It was so windy. Windy like it is today. Windy just like this.

(He removes a newspaper from the back of the wheel chair, unfolds it and begins to read. The light around

him dims slightly. The light on The **WOMAN** *becomes very bright. After a pause, she slowly rises from her wheelchair, steps out of it and moves to stand behind him.)*

WOMAN. Why doesn't he know I'm fine? I'm fine in here.

(She puts her hand on his shoulder.)

Why did I ever think conversation is what binds people to one another? That's wrong. It's the silences that bind us. I had to get here to know that.

It's true that enormous chunks of me have broken off and disappeared. Like pieces of ice from an iceberg. But some things stay as they always were.

For instance, there's a dream I have, over and over. It never varies. I'm running, toward the edge of a cliff, and I'm going so fast I can't stop, and I'm scared because I know I'm going to slip off it.

And I do. I do slip off the edge. I am catapulted, and I go tumbling headlong, and I somersault, and there's no bottom, and there's no top, and there's no time, and then suddenly, the wind makes a sound, a kind of "whoosh," and there is this…silence.

So deep. Cool on my cheek. Smelling like clean laundry.

I dive into it. I bob up and down in waves of silence. I jump and play in silence, like a dolphin in the ocean. And it's not a prison. And in the dream I'm not afraid. In the dream I'm not afraid of the last word.

(The **WOMAN** *begins to dance, slowly at first, making big, wide circles.)*

I'm not afraid.

(She dances faster and faster. She is spinning like a Sufi now, full of twirling and buoyancy and joy. The **MAN** *continues to read the paper to himself. The* **WOMAN** *dances into the darkness of the stage as the lights fade.)*

www.ingramcontent.com/pod-product-compliance
Lightning Source LLC
Chambersburg PA
CBHW071414290426
44108CB00014B/1813